My First Animal Library

Mice

by Martha E. H. Rustad

Ideas for Parents and Teachers

Bullfrog Books let children practice reading informational texts at the earliest reading levels. Repetition, familiar words, and photo labels support early readers.

Before Reading
- Discuss the cover photo. What does it tell them?
- Look at the picture glossary together. Read and discuss the words.

Read the Book
- "Walk" through the book and look at the photos. Let the child ask questions. Point out the photo labels.
- Read the book to the child, or have him or her read independently.

After Reading
- Prompt the child to think more. Ask: Have you ever seen a mouse? Where was it? What was it doing?

Bullfrog Books are published by Jump!
5357 Penn Avenue South
Minneapolis, MN 55419
www.jumplibrary.com

Library of Congress Cataloging-in-Publication Data
Rustad, Martha E. H. (Martha Elizabeth Hillman), 1975-
  Mice / by Martha E.H. Rustad.
    p. cm. -- (Bullfrog books. My first animal library, nocturnal animals)
  Summary: "This easy-to-read nonfiction story tells a "night in the life" of a mouse, from waking up, finding food and feeding babies, to going back to sleep when the sun comes up"-- Provided by publisher.
  Audience: 005.
  Audience: K to grade 3.
  Includes bibliographical references and index.
  ISBN 978-1-62031-070-0 (hardcover) -- ISBN 978-1-62496-070-3 (ebook)
  1. Mice--Juvenile literature. I. Title.
  QL737.R6R87 2014
  599.35'3--dc23
                                        2013004609

Series Editor: Rebecca Glaser
Series Designer: Ellen Huber
Book Designer: Danny Nanos

Photo Credits: All photos by Shutterstock except the following: Alamy 14, 16-17, 18-19, 21, 23tr, 23bl; Corbis 23tl; Dreamstime 9

Printed in the United States at Corporate Graphics in North Mankato, Minnesota.

5-2013 / PO 1003
10 9 8 7 6 5 4 3 2 1

Table of Contents

Mice at Night

The sun sets.

Night begins.

Mice wake up.

A mouse peeks out into the dark.

It sniffs.

It listens.

7

Long whiskers feel the air.

whiskers

8

The mouse is safe.
It sneaks out quietly.

The mouse
finds food.

It eats nuts, bugs,
and berries.

It stores food
near its nest.

Hiss! A snake!

Snakes like to eat mice.

The mouse runs away fast.

It hides in a hole.

Mice gnaw holes in wood.
They have strong teeth.

teeth

Some mice make tunnels in houses.

Tunnels lead to nests.

Baby mice stay in the nest.

They are called pups.

pup

17

Squeak! Squeak!
The pups are hungry.
Mama mouse has milk.
She feeds all her pups
at once.

The sun rises.

Day begins.

Mice go to sleep.

Parts of a Mouse

ears
Big ears help mice listen for quiet sounds.

fur
Mice are mammals.

teeth
Strong teeth help mice gnaw through wood.

whiskers
Mice feel their surroundings with their whiskers.

Picture Glossary

gnaw
To chew and chew on something.

store
To save up something to use later; mice store food.

pup
A young mouse.

tunnel
A long, narrow passage dug through something.

Index

To Learn More

Learning more is as easy as 1, 2, 3.

1) Go to www.factsurfer.com

2) Enter "mice" into the search box.

3) Click the "Surf" button to see a list of websites.

With factsurfer.com, finding more information is just a click away.

06/14